Thanks, *Mom*

Inspiration for a Mother's Heart

Thanks, *Mom*

Inspiration for a Mother's Heart

BARBOUR
PUBLISHING

Scripture quotations marked KJV are taken from the King James Version of the Bible.

Scripture quotations marked NIV are taken from the HOLY BIBLE, NEW INTERNATIONAL VERSION®. NIV®. Copyright © 1973, 1978, 1984 by International Bible Society. Used by permission of Zondervan. All rights reserved.

Scripture quotations marked NKJV are taken from the New King James Version®. Copyright © 1982 by Thomas Nelson, Inc. Used by permission. All rights reserved.

Scripture quotations marked TEV are from the Today's English Version—Second Edition, Copyright © 1992 by American Bible Society. Used by permission.

Scripture quotations marked MSG are taken from *THE MESSAGE*. Copyright © by Eugene H. Peterson 1993, 1994, 1995, 1996, 2000, 2001, 2002. Used by permission of Nav Press Publishing Group.

Cover image © Diane Macdonald/Photographer's Choice/Getty Images

Published by Barbour Publishing, Inc., P.O. Box 719, Uhrichsville, Ohio 44683, www.barbourbooks.com

Our mission is to publish and distribute inspirational products offering exceptional value and biblical encouragement to the masses.

Member of the
Evangelical Christian
Publishers Association

Printed in China.

Contents

Thanks, Mom!

But we were gentle among you, like a mother caring for her little children.

1 Thessalonians 2:7 NIV

Mothers are truly a gift from God, a physical expression of His love. Celebrate your role as "Mom" with this joyous collection of devotional selections, scriptures, quotations, and prayers. This book is a great big "Thank you!" for all that you do and all that you are to your family.

A Mother's Care
and Compassion

As a mother comforts her child,
so will I comfort you.

ISAIAH 66:13 NIV

IF YOU WANT JOY

*J*ust as the simple presence of the mother makes the child's joy, so does the simple fact of God's presence make our joy. The mother may not make a single promise to the child nor explain any of her plans or purposes, but she is, and that is enough for the child. And to the child, there is behind all that changes and can change the one unchangeable joy of the mother's existence. While the mother lives, the child will be cared for; the child knows this, instinctively if not intelligently, and rejoices in knowing it. And to the children of God, as well, there is behind all that changes and can change the one unchangeable joy that God is. And while He is, His children will be cared for, and they ought to know it and rejoice in it, as instinctively as and far more intelligently than the child of human parents. For what else can God do, being what He is? Neglect, indifference, forgetfulness, ignorance are all impossible to Him. He knows everything, He cares about everything, He can manage everything, and He loves us! Surely this is enough for a "fullness of joy" beyond the power of words to express, no matter what else may be missed besides.

HANNAH WHITALL SMITH

A mother's arms are made of tenderness,
and children sleep soundly in them.

Victor Hugo

REACHING OUT

*Y*ou know, Father, sometimes I'm guilty of feeling sorry for myself, but when I stop and really think about why I'm complaining, I realize that I have much to be thankful for. There are so many people who really do need a listening ear or a heartfelt hug.

Often, Lord, it's my own children who need a mother's compassionate arms. It's sometimes hard to reach out to others, including my kids, because I feel so vulnerable. I'm afraid I'll say or do the wrong thing. But You want me to extend myself to the hurting individuals in this world, and I know You'll show me what to do.

Please, Father, help me to never turn down an opportunity to offer compassion.

RACHEL QUILLIN AND NANCY J. FARRIER

They that sow in tears shall reap in joy.

PSALM 126:5 KJV

A JOYFUL HARVEST

The home is a greenhouse; the mother, a gardener.

Like a good gardener, a mother prepares the home soil with encouragement, compassion, and good home cooking so that each of her plants will grow strong and true.

She nourishes their bodies, souls, and spirits, always considering the needs of each tender seedling. One may need extra love; another, extra patience; another, laughter.

She guards her plants jealously, praying always for their protection from dangerous friendships, poor choices, and other weeds that threaten to choke life from them.

Yet despite her faithfulness, she cannot control their growth. Some flourish with little effort, while others need more attention. As she labors, she often becomes weary and worn. She sweats and cries over them, praying always that the Master Gardener will water them with wisdom and truth.

Often when He does intervene, the mother-gardener is tried. Her vines may be pruned or her seedlings transplanted. Sometimes He'll allow weeds to grow, and it's all she can do to keep her hands away, to stay out of the marvelous work that He is doing.

But she trusts the hand of the Master Gardener.

And waits for a joyful harvest.

HELEN WIDGER MIDDLEBROOKE

There are only two lasting bequests we can hope to give our children. One is roots; and the other, wings.

HODDING CARTER

Making a Difference

What a long way a little compassion goes, dear Jesus. Sometimes I think that all I need is a hug to make me feel better. I'm sure that others out there feel the same way. It's obvious that my kids often do.

Just the other day, my little one hurt himself. I was busy and could have easily told him to sit and rest a few minutes and he'd be okay. Physically that might have been true, but he would have only become frustrated. What a joy it was for me to sit with him and to see the healing powers of a mother's compassion. How quickly he recovered!

Lord, sometimes compassion is all a person needs to gain strength. I pray I will always offer it freely.

Rachel Quillin and Nancy J. Farrier

And of some have compassion,
making a difference.

A Mother's Encouragement

Yet I was the one who taught Israel to walk. I took my people up in my arms. . . . I drew them to me with affection and love. I picked them up and held them to my cheek.

HOSEA 11:3–4 TEV

PATIENT ENCOURAGEMENT

*T*eaching a young child a new skill takes love, patience, and a very positive attitude. The toddler can become discouraged as he tries to fold his clothes, make his bed, or even learn to use a spoon to feed himself. Each new experience is a chance to encourage our preschooler.

When he makes a mistake, his mother can make the difference in his learning experience. As mothers we can chastise or show anger and impatience, sending a message to the child that he isn't worthy of our love and time. However, when we demonstrate our love by helping him try again, our toddler will blossom and grow to his full potential. He will learn to trust us and his learned abilities.

When we become Christians, God is the One who teaches us to be like Him. His love encompasses us. If we feel worthless after making a mistake, that emotion doesn't come from God. He pulls us to Him and holds us close. He uses affection to urge us to try again. His love and patience toward us are beyond expression.

Nancy J. Farrier

The mother's heart is the child's classroom.

HENRY WARD BEECHER

HOLDING HANDS

*F*ather, You've held my hand and helped me in some difficult situations. With Your help, I've walked when I might have fallen.

Not once have You ever laughed at me or told me how silly I was to be fearful. Lord, sometimes the things my children are uncertain about seem so unimportant to me. I struggle not to laugh. Help me to be understanding, to encourage rather than discourage. I want to take their hands and walk with them, as You've taken mine to walk with me.

RACHEL QUILLIN AND NANCY J. FARRIER

You therefore, my son, be strong in the grace that is in Christ Jesus.

2 TIMOTHY 2:1 NKJV

Strength in Grace

The young mother watched her child take his first hesitant steps. After tumbling to the ground, his eyes turned to his mother, seeking her reaction. Her bright smile and obvious joy at his success, not his fall, encouraged the child to try again. Each time he tried, he grew stronger. Before long the child's steps were no longer hesitant but confident.

By not displaying anger or concern but showing understanding and encouragement, the mother gave her son the strength to climb back up and try again. The boy trusted her for his well-being. He continued to learn to walk and then to run.

As Christians we often fall or make mistakes. God's grace is always there to demonstrate His forgiveness. He urges us to climb to our feet and try again. Every time we attempt to walk in faith, we are resting in God's grace and drawing strength from Him. On our own, we would fall and not be able to try again. With God in charge of our well-being, we can have not only the ability to walk, but we can learn to run with confidence in God as well.

Nancy J. Farrier

My mother said to me, "If you become a soldier, you'll be a general; if you become a monk, you'll end up as the pope." Instead I became a painter and wound up as Picasso.

PABLO PICASSO

26

HELD IN GOD'S HAND

*F*ather, I don't have to depend on my strength, because You give me Yours, Lord, and You never run out. I can picture You holding me up as the difficulties press close. You help me when there is no one else to do so.

Thank You, Lord. I'm grateful that I can show my children where to turn in times of trouble. They don't have to try to do it all themselves, because we are all Your children. You care for us all and will carry us when times are tough. I praise You, Lord.

RACHEL QUILLIN AND NANCY J. FARRIER

"Let the little children come to me; do not stop them. . . ." And he took them up in his arms, laid his hands on them, and blessed them.

MARK 10:14, 16 NRSV

A Mother's
Generosity

"Give, and it will be given to you."

LUKE 6:38 NIV

ALL OUR NEEDS

Doesn't it feel good to give? As moms, we're programmed to give. We give up our figures to carry babies in our bellies. We give up yoga classes for Baby and Me sessions. We give up golf for playgroup time. We give up sleep for nightly feedings. We give up a lot! But we also get much in return.

In one of my favorite movies called *The Thrill of It All*, starring Doris Day and James Garner, there's a great line describing motherhood. James Garner plays Dr. Boyer, an adorable obstetrician, and one of his patients says to him, "I don't know when I've been so happy. I guess there's nothing more fulfilling in life than having a baby."

I suppose that's true, although there are days when we haven't had a shower or any sleep that we might question that statement! Being a mother is a great honor and an awesome undertaking. It requires a great deal of giving—giving love, giving praise, giving encouragement, giving spankings, giving wisdom—giving it all! But we don't have to go it alone. On the days when we have nothing left to give, God does. He will supply all our needs. He will give to us so that we can give to our families.

MICHELLE MEDLOCK ADAMS

Mother's love grows by giving.

CHARLES LAMB

GIVE

*Y*ou've made it plenty clear, Lord, that giving is a command—not an option. You've also made it plain what the results of obedience to this command will be. Father, I have so many good opportunities to give. I already know that I'm to give my tithe to the church. I can give beyond that as You speak to my heart and provide the finances.

And I can give more than money. I can find ways to serve in the church or just to spend extra time nurturing my children. Lord, You told me to give and that, if I do, it shall be given to me. You don't say what "it" is, but Your generosity is unmatched and Your blessings are always wonderful. Thank You!

RACHEL QUILLIN AND NANCY J. FARRIER

So we say with confidence, "The Lord is my helper; I will not be afraid."

HEBREWS 13:6 NIV

Up to Any Challenge

*W*hat's on your agenda today? Are you facing some big challenges? No matter what you're going to be up against today, God's got you covered. He says in Hebrews that He will be your helper. You don't have to be afraid.

I don't know about you, but I sometimes feel afraid. Sure, I put on a good outward appearance, but on the inside I feel insecure. I wonder if I'm doing a good enough job as a mom. Do you ever wonder if you're measuring up? I especially feel that way when I am around moms who are doing everything right. You know, the really cool mom who has a clean house, all of her laundry folded and put away, no dirty dishes in the sink *ever*, well-mannered children, and a perfect figure, too! I want to be a mom like that someday.

But until then, I am declaring that "I will not be afraid." God did not give us a spirit of fear, but of love and of power and of sound mind. We are up to any challenge. We can do all things through Him. We can be confident in Him today and every day.

Michelle Medlock Adams

You may have others who will be more demonstrative but never who will love you more unselfishly than your mother or who will be willing to do or bear more for your good.

CATHERINE BRAMWELL BOOTH

MEETING NEEDS

*F*ather, there are many people in this world who are needy. Some lack the basic necessities of life, such as food and clothing. Others lack time or friendship. Open my eyes to the needs of others, and guide me to reach out to people as You give me the opportunities.

I try to teach my children to share. What better way is there to do that than to give them an example? And who knows? Maybe someday it will be me or one of my children who is in need. I would be much more content to receive help from others if I knew that, when I'd had the chance, I had reached out to them.

Instill in me a generous spirit, Lord.

RACHEL QUILLIN AND NANCY J. FARRIER

He that watereth shall be watered also himself.

PROVERBS 11:25 KJV

A Mother's
Guidance

"Build up, build up, prepare the road! Remove the obstacles out of the way of my people."

ISAIAH 57:14 NIV

GROWING UP, LETTING GO

I can do it by myself!"

"I know you can, honey, but Mommy just wants to help you."

"I don't need your help!"

I've dreamed of this moment for years—the time when the girls would actually start doing more for themselves. But now something just does not feel quite right.

This vague feeling of loss is a continuous process. From their infancy until the present, our children's level of dependency on [their father] and me has changed dramatically.

As parents, we knew this would happen. In fact, we prayed that our children would grow up to be strong, independent adults. But it still isn't easy to let go.

I'll never forget Laura's first day of school. My legs were like lead as I left her in a classroom of near strangers. My vision was cloudy with tears, and I knew I had to get out of there fast before everyone saw Laura's mommy cry like a baby.

Of course when Mary starts "big school," I'll experience it all over again, but that's all right. All these little "letting go's" are preparing me for the big ones later on. And I know that when the day arrives and the girls walk away into college, marriage, or a career, I'll feel pretty much the same way. And I'll breathe pretty much the same prayer: "Oh God, how I love these girls. . .please take care of them for us!"

LEIGH ANN THOMAS

The successful mother, the mother who does her part in rearing and training aright the boys and girls who are to be the men and women of the next generation, is of greater use to the community. . . . She is more important by far than the successful statesman or businessman or artist or scientist.

THEODORE ROOSEVELT

TEACH ME TO PARENT

Thank You for my children, Lord. They are my most precious gifts from You. I look at them and see how they reflect different family members—their hair, their eyes, the little dimple like mine. Most of all, I pray they will have Your eyes and learn the wonders of Your ways.

Help me teach my children the lessons in Your Word. Remind me to talk about Your scriptures in our home. May this become a way of life. Through the years, I pray my dear ones will learn to apply Your lessons to all they do.

When I must discipline, grant me love, strength, and consistency. Let me lead them into a life of love, responsibility, truth, and hope for the future. Grant me understanding as I work with each child, so I won't be too strict or too lenient. Help me develop love and security in them, rather than fear and anger. Let everything I do be out of loving action, not reaction.

I can't think of a job more challenging than meeting the needs of my children. I can only do it through You, my Lord. Go before me, I pray. As I endeavor to do Your will, I petition Your help. Enable me to train up my children in the way they should go, so when they are older, they will remain close to You. In Jesus' name I pray. Amen.

ANITA CORRINE DONIHUE

The older women. . .can train the younger women to love their husbands and children, to be self-controlled and pure, to be busy at home, to be kind.

TITUS 2:3–5 NIV

My Mother

*I*f my mother had been a different woman, I would be a different person. When she read to me each night, I learned about the world of words; today I make my living writing—and I still love coming home from the library with a stack of books to keep me company. When my mother took me outdoors and named the trees and flowers and birds for me, I learned about the world of nature. Today, whenever I'm upset or discouraged, I still find peace walking in the woods, and when I recognize ash and beech, trillium and hepatica, purple finches and indigo buntings, I feel as though I'm saying the names of dear, old friends. And when my mother prayed with me each night and before each meal, I learned about an eternal world; today I seek God's presence daily and offer up my life to Him in prayer.

My mother trained me well.

Ellyn Sanna

*My mother was the most beautiful woman
I ever saw. All I am I owe to my mother.
I attribute all my success in life to the
moral, intellectual, and physical education
I received from her.*

GEORGE WASHINGTON

JESUS IN ME

*D*ear Father God, You are the best example of what a loving parent should be. I know I am called to be Christlike in all I do, and that includes my parenting methods.

Please give me the strength and the wisdom to be the godly example that my children need to see. I know that the life I live will have a profound influence on the attitudes my children develop concerning You.

I want to be instrumental in helping my kids establish a close walk with You. I realize that in order for this to happen I must be like You. Direct me daily to renew my commitment to follow in Your steps. Thank You for being the example I need.

RACHEL QUILLIN AND NANCY J. FARRIER

I will behave myself wisely in a perfect way. O when wilt thou come unto me? I will walk within my house with a perfect heart.

PSALM 101:2 KJV

A Mother's Love
and Sacrifice

"By this all men will know that you are my disciples, if you love one another."

JOHN 13:35 NIV

REFLECTED LOVE

*B*ecause God's love is reflected in ours, our children will learn about God simply through motherhood's love. Oh, we need to teach our children about God and His Word. We need to read them Bible stories and pray with them, answer their questions, and take them to church. We need to live in such a way that they'll see what it means to be a Christian. But on a much more basic level, they'll understand about a God who always hears, because when they were babies, we responded to their cries. They'll be able to have faith in a God who meets their needs, because we saw that they never went hungry. God's strength and tenderness will be real to them because they caught a glimpse of it in our love, from the time they were born.

So, mothers, never let the world tell you that what you do is not important. Remember, when you rock your babies and sing a lullaby, your arms and voice are God's. When you do load after load of dirty diapers, then grass-stained play clothes, and finally school clothes smeared with ketchup and chocolate pudding, remember: Your hands are God's hands. And when you love your children unconditionally, all the way from colic to adolescent rebellion, you are loving with God's love. Through you, He will imprint Himself on your children's hearts.

ELLYN SANNA

*Mother is the name for God in the lips
and hearts of little children.*

WILLIAM MAKEPEACE THACKERAY

SACRIFICIAL LOVE

*T*hank You, Jesus, for Your sacrificial love for me. Thank You also for the example of true love that You have provided.

Lord, true love often requires giving of one's self. I'm learning where that might be true in parenting. Having children has brought about many changes in my life. They've all been worthwhile, but that doesn't mean they've all been easy. A certain amount of freedom had to be surrendered. My schedule had to be renovated in order to meet the demands of my children. Even basic tasks like grocery shopping have a new level of difficulty. But these changes are so worthwhile when I look at the happy smiles on my children's faces or feel their little arms around my neck. Love is beautiful!

RACHEL QUILLIN AND NANCY J. FARRIER

Walk in love, as Christ also hath loved us, and hath given himself for us an offering and a sacrifice to God for a sweetsmelling savour.

EPHESIANS 5:2 KJV

I HAVE OTHER THINGS TO DO

I have other things to do. . . .too much to get finished before bed-time.

But here I am, with a baby on my lap, going round and round and up and down on a carousel. Behind me, my six-year-old lectures his younger brother and sister about merry-go-rounds and carousels, about horse tails and whatever else captures his fleeting fancy. . . . The kids get off the ride with new energy, eager to explore.

"Let's go to the castle! . . ." They have been to this park countless times, but to them it is new again. After all, it is a new day.

I watch them wistfully. Oh, to have the eyes of a child to see the world afresh each day! To have a child's mind that neither lingers on the past nor frets about the future. . . .

To children, life is "now." And they are right. Life is now. We are promised nothing beyond this moment. Marriage and motherhood—and childhood—are not forever but for now. Yet if we miss them now, we will have missed them forever.

They run to the playground near the mill.

"Mommy! Watch me!"

"Mommy! Push me!"

I lift my preschooler into the swing and give a push.

"I'm thwinging!" she laughs. "Higher!"

I give another push. And another.

Yes, I have other things to do.

But none better.

HELEN WIDGER MIDDLEBROOKE

God loves us the way a good mother loves—totally, unconditionally, with a nurturing and ever-present care. In fact, as mothers, our love for our children is only a dim reflection of the love God has for His people.

ELLYN SANNA

SPECIAL DAYS

*L*ord, I collapse onto our couch, kick my shoes off, and think of today's blessings. Family and friends bustled around. Children chattered with youthful excitement. Steaming irresistible food simmered in the kitchen. Men exchanged stories and (thank You, Lord) helped with the little ones. It seems a whooshing dream; the day went so fast.

I reflect briefly on the struggles we've all had, the mountains we've fearfully conquered with Your help. Still we're together, loving and sharing. It was worth listening to each other and finding Your will through the years. I'm tired, but I loved it all. At nightfall little arms wrapped around my neck with an "I love you, Nana." Strong embraces from sons so dear and tender hugs from loving daughters filled my heart with joy.

I thank You, Lord, for this day that You created and for the love of family and friends. As special days end in all their wild flurry, I'm often reminded of the true value in it all, not food, fancies, and elaborations but my dearest friends and loved ones.

She watches over the affairs of her household and does not eat the bread of idleness. Her children arise and call her blessed; her husband also, and he praises her.

PROVERBS 31:27–28 NIV

A Mother's
Patience

Be cheerful no matter what; pray all the time; thank God no matter what happens. This is the way God wants you who belong to Christ Jesus to live.

1 THESSALONIANS 5:16–18 MSG

Under Construction

*S*urely, when God said to give thanks for everything, He didn't mean the time when the baby had the stomach flu and shared the virus with the entire family. He couldn't have been thinking of when we had to scrub an unidentifiable stickiness off the new carpet. Or when the dog chewed up the TV remote.

This parenting gig is a long and exasperating process at times. Often it seems as if so much of what we do is routine, mundane, or just plain hard.

But God didn't qualify His biblical admonishment of giving thanks in all things. He really meant all things! Every circumstance in our life—annoying, frustrating, even ordinary moments.

God notices those moments! He cares about them. He promises to never leave or forsake us, even in the middle of the night when the baby has a dirty diaper. Or scraping off a half-eaten Pop-tart from the car seat.

Giving thanks reminds us that what really matters is what's going on inside of us. God is at work, fixing, renewing, cleaning up our mess. Our patience is growing, our kindness is stretching, our love is being made perfect. At all times, we're in process and under construction.

Suzanne Woods Fisher

A mother's patience is like a tube of toothpaste—it's never quite gone.

UNKNOWN

HEAR MY CRY

What a rich promise in Psalm 40:1, Lord! If I wait patiently, You will listen and hear my cry. Psalm 40:2 talks about being in miry clay. How many times have my troubles dragged me down like clinging clay, yet You were there to rescue me!

Put a new song in my mouth, Lord. Let my children see me being patient and waiting on You, no matter what the difficulty I'm facing. Help them learn the same song of joy that You are giving me. Together we can sing Your praises to all those around us. You hear us, Lord. You are our mighty Savior.

When I learn to be patient and trust in You, I know that You will hear my cries and I will be blessed. Thank You for this blessing.

RACHEL QUILLIN AND NANCY J. FARRIER

But if we have food and clothing, we will be content with that.

1 TIMOTHY 6:8 NIV

CHOSEN SATISFACTION

The mother sighed and closed her eyes, fighting impatience. Her child had whined all day. Nothing had satisfied her. She wondered again if her daughter was coming down with something. Every time the girl was tired or getting sick, she was impossible to please. Even if she asked for her favorite snack, by the time it was ready, the preschooler didn't want to eat it.

Picking up her child, the mother held her close. Normally she was a delight and easy to care for. The mother began to rock, hoping her daughter would forget her discomfort. The girl relaxed against her.

We are often cranky with God. The weather is too hot or too cold. Nobody likes us. We don't have enough money. People expect us to do everything. Work is piling up, and we don't have time to get our chores done. The complaints are endless.

Being satisfied, or content, is a choice. Our focus has to change from ourselves to God. We have to remember all He has done and given us. Often the worst times of discontent are when we are tired, sick, or our routine is somehow thrown off. Each time we must choose to focus on God and be satisfied with Him. We can lean back and relax in His arms.

NANCY J. FARRIER

Mother: The person who sits up with you when you are sick and puts up with you when you are well.

UNKNOWN

HAPPINESS THROUGH ENDURANCE

*W*hine. Whine. Whine. That's all I seem to do, Lord. I'm sure You get tired of me never being satisfied. When things are going well, I complain about not growing spiritually. When things are going wrong, I complain about the trial. How can You still love me when I'm so weak and impatient to be more like You?

Today I was unpleasant with the children. They were whining because they all wanted their own way. I saw myself reflected in them. Then I thought of the prophets and realized how my troubles are nothing compared to theirs.

Still my complaining heart, Lord. Fill me with rejoicing. You are refining me. I want to teach my children patience by my own example. Give me strength for the task.

RACHEL QUILLIN AND NANCY J. FARRIER

Behold, we count them happy which endure. Ye have heard of the patience of Job, and have seen the end of the Lord; that the Lord is very pitiful, and of tender mercy.

JAMES 5:11 KJV

A Mother's Prayers

In the morning, O LORD, *you hear my voice; in the morning I lay my requests before you and wait in expectation.*

PSALM 5:3 NIV

Our Prayer Requests

*W*hen my children were young, the only way I could ensure having a special quiet time of prayer was to get up earlier than anyone else in the house. On weekdays this translated to 5:30 a.m. Settled into one particular chair, I read my Bible and then prayed for each member of our family. Although I never made a big deal about this habit, occasionally the kids would catch a glimpse of me there as they began their own busy days.

On Sunday evenings I would ask my husband and children for any particular things they'd like me to pray about that week. Such concerns as tests, projects, or schoolwork that were due, and once in awhile class bullies or teachers were voiced. (Whenever "teachers" came up, I figured my child had been given a great deal of homework and resented it.)

Often in the morning I'd find little folded notes on my prayer chair. Now that our children are raised, I wish I'd saved some of those crumpled "last-minute additions" always written on notebook paper. But I do have memories of the celebrating we did when one of those prayers was answered.

Are you laying your own requests before the Lord?

Carol L. Fitzpatrick

All that I am or hope to be, I owe to my angel mother. I remember my mother's prayers, and they have always followed me. They have clung to me all my life.

ABRAHAM LINCOLN

God Is Always Available

Thank You, Father, that You are never too busy for me. That's hard for me to fathom, because so often I hear myself saying to my kids, "Just give me a minute. I have to get this done." And it's true, Lord. I really can't be totally available to all of my children every minute of every day.

But, Lord, You are always willing to hear my petitions, no matter what the time of day. It doesn't matter if multitudes of other people are bringing requests before You at the same instant. You are God, and You will hear and answer each of us.

Remind me that You really do want me to come before You all day long. And please help me to be more available to my own children.

Rachel Quillin and Nancy J. Farrier

For this child I prayed; and the Lord hath given me my petition which I asked of him: Therefore also I have lent him to the Lord; as long as he liveth he shall be lent to the Lord.

1 SAMUEL 1:27–28 KJV

A HANNAH HEART

*I*n her sorrow of barrenness, Hannah prayed for a son and promised him back to God. When God answered her prayer, Hannah kept her word.

She gave Samuel back to the Lord when he was just a boy. Instead of keeping him by her side, as most mothers would, Hannah left Samuel in the care of an old prophet who couldn't control his own children.

Hannah had a heart of faith, as her song of praise in 1 Samuel 2 shows. She knew the God who had given her a son could and would protect him.

Hannah also had a heart to worship, and she taught her small son to do the same. Scripture says he worshipped before Eli instructed him. Apparently his mother had instilled a fear of God in him and shown him how to respond.

Oh, to have a heart of faith and worship!

Then we would take our babies to church despite any criticism, and we would not fear when our children head off to some forgotten mission field.

Lord, give us hearts that trust.

Give us Hannah hearts!

HELEN WIDGER MIDDLEBROOKE

Instead of fretting, my mother prayed and committed me into God's hands. She gained comfort knowing that God watched over me at all times and in every situation.

SHERYL LYNN HILL

I Prayed for a Child

Thank You for granting my request and blessing me with a beautiful family. Lord, as Hannah did, I give my children back to You. My prayer now is that each of my children would accept You as their personal Savior. Then I ask that You would use each one for Your glory.

Help my children to dedicate themselves to serving You in whatever capacity You would call them. Be with them as they face the many temptations that abound. Show them what convictions to establish and give them the strength to stand firm in those convictions. Please protect them from spiritual and physical harm, and give them sound minds and bodies.

I thank You in advance for answered prayers.

Rachel Quillin and Nancy J. Farrier

Evening, and morning, and at noon,
will I pray, and cry aloud: and he
shall hear my voice.

PSALM 55:17 KJV

A Mother's Trust
and Understanding

Thou wilt shew me the path of life: in thy presence is fulness of joy; at thy right hand there are pleasures for evermore.

PSALM 16:11 KJV

Sweetest and Best

A Christian lady. . .was once expressing to a friend how impossible she found it to say, "Thy will be done," and how afraid she should be to do it. She was the mother of an only little boy who was the heir to a great fortune and the idol of her heart. After she had stated her difficulties fully, her friend said, "Suppose your little Charley should come running to you tomorrow and say, 'Mother, I am always going to obey you, and I will trust your love.' How would you feel towards him? Would you say to yourself, 'Ah, now I shall have a chance to make Charley miserable. I will take away all his pleasures and fill his life with every hard and disagreeable thing that I can find. I will compel him to do just the things that are the most difficult for him to do and will give him all sorts of impossible commands.'" "Oh, no, no, no!" exclaimed the indignant mother. "You know I would not. You know I would hug him to my heart and cover him with kisses and would hasten to fill his life with all that was sweetest and best." "And are you more tender and more loving than God?"

Hannah Whitall Smith

Mother means selfless devotion, limitless sacrifice, and love that passes understanding.

UNKNOWN

WITH THE WHOLE HEART

*L*ord, I want to trust You. I give all my cares to You and try to walk away, but so often I fail. I begin to reason with myself. Then I begin to fear and doubt. I snatch back all my cares, as if I am more trustworthy than You.

Forgive me, Lord. I don't want to do this anymore. I want to trust You completely—with my children, with my life. Letting You have total control is easy to say and so hard to do. I feel like I'm walking in the dark, not knowing which way You're leading me.

That doesn't matter, though. I know I can trust You with my whole heart. You alone are worthy. I give it all to You, Lord.

RACHEL QUILLIN AND NANCY J. FARRIER

Above all, love each other deeply.

1 PETER 4:8 NIV

Hearts Entwined Forever

When my daughter Emily was little, she was my constant companion. Her little chattering voice brought new life to everything I did. Once, waiting in an examination room, the two of us were talking a blue streak when the nurse came in. "You two are best buddies, aren't you?" she said. And we were.

When Emily went to preschool, I gave her a gold heart of mine to wear, to remind her that my love went with her. When I went into the hospital for the birth of my second child, she gave it back to remind me that her love would be with me. And when she went to kindergarten, I bought her a duplicate necklace, so that she would know she was always in my heart.

But as she grew older and my life got busier, I sometimes worried that I would lose her, that she would disappear into her own new world of school and friends, and I would never recover the person who had been such a good companion to me.

As she becomes a young woman instead of a child, I find we relate to each other in a new way. Now, as we have woman-to-woman talks, I realize she's still a good companion. And yesterday, as she was hurrying off to meet her friends, I noticed the small gold heart that glittered at her throat. I touched the gold heart around my own neck and smiled.

Ellyn Sanna

Everybody knows that a good mother gives her children a feeling of trust and stability. She is the one they can count on for the things that matter most of all.

KATHARINE BUTLER HATHAWAY

Brought Together in Love

Comfort my heart. Give me full understanding and assurance. In this family of Christ, I should be feeling rich in love and compassion. Instead, some of the people are critical of me or of my children, and that hurts, Lord.

To be honest, there are many times I'm critical, too, and I'm reminded that it is my pride that usually causes me to criticize others. These people are my family, Lord. By finding fault in them, I'm setting a poor example of how to belong.

True love is kind, not prideful or self-seeking. Fill me with compassion for my fellow Christians so I might be a godly example of love and understanding. I want to emulate You, Jesus.

Rachel Quillin and Nancy J. Farrier

That their hearts might be comforted, being knit together in love, and unto all riches of the full assurance of understanding, to the acknowledgment of the mystery of God, and of the Father, and of Christ.

COLOSSIANS 2:2 KJV

A Mother's
Wisdom

From the lips of children and infants you have ordained praise.

PSALM 8:2 NIV

THROUGH LITTLE EYES

Before each child entered the crawl-around stage, I would crawl on all fours to "childproof" our home. As the girls have grown, I've realized that babyhood isn't the only time that it's important to look through a child's eyes.

Sometimes we moms are so busy that we forget our children have quite a lot to teach us—if we'll take the time to learn. Quite often what seems ordinary to us becomes spectacular from a child's perspective.

My friend Holly and her daughter were admiring a full moon when Mary Cate announced with three-year-old wonder, "Look, Mama, the moon has all its pieces!" With a smile and a hug, the moment was sealed in that mother's heart for all time.

Children remind us to laugh, no—giggle. They help us rediscover the simple joys of the sun on our face and grass under bare feet.

But even more important, children teach us about God. They show us how to pray believing and how to live abundantly. They take their heavenly Father at His word, and they expect us to do the same.

What happiness God must feel when His little messengers reach the heart of an adult! For surely He is pleased when we remember to take joy in loving Him, in just being His child.

LEIGH ANN THOMAS

A child's hand in yours—what tenderness and power it arouses. You are instantly the very touchstone of wisdom and strength.

MARJORIE HOLMES

Our Children

The house rumbles with laughter and tussles. I hurry to keep up with it all. They are a heritage that comes from You, Lord. These bursts of energy in various sizes and personalities are like arrows in a warrior's hands.

I call on You for wisdom. Each day I thank You for guidance in handling different situations. Thank You, Lord, for how You help me teach our children about Your love. I treasure Your leading as I share Your lessons with them while we go about our activities at home, when we share walks, as we pray together at bedtime and rise each morning to face a new day.

My husband and I have dedicated our lives and these children to You, Lord. I know for sure Your hand is and will be upon them throughout their entire lives. I write Your words on plaques, pictures, and on our doorposts that "As for me and my household, we will serve the LORD" (Joshua 24:15 NIV).

Anita Corrine Donihue

*The living, the living—they praise you,
as I am doing today; fathers tell their
children about your faithfulness.*

ISAIAH 38:19 NIV

THE PRESENT

"There's no time like the present."

That's what my mother always used to say when she wanted me to clean my room. Now I find myself using that very same line on my girls. Of course, they look at me the same way I used to look at my mom when she used that expression on me. (Yes, I rolled my eyes at my mom, too!) Still, the fact remains that it's a true statement. There really is no time like the present.

So, if there is something you've been longing to do, or someplace you've been dreaming of going, or someone you've been wanting to visit—go for it. Do it today. Seize the moment! What are you waiting for?

We're not promised tomorrow, which is why we need to live each day as if it were our last. Love a little more. Laugh a little more. Hug your kids more. Serve God with all your heart. Don't let the sun go down without telling your family how much you love them. Make sure your kids know how much Jesus loves them. Think of today as a gift from God—because it is.

Michelle Medlock Adams

As we live [God's] abundant life, interested in His world and delighting ourselves in all the tiny blessings He sends our way, we will find that we are beautiful and fulfilled simply because we are God's.

ELLYN SANNA